The Storm

Michael R Lewis

ISBN:0990368106
ISBN-13:9780990368106

DEDICATION

To my parents Jimmy and Velta and my brother Randy who weathered the
Storm and survived.

CONTENTS

ACKNOWLEDGMENTS

This book would not have been possible without the support and advice of my brother Randy, my wife, and my children.

My editor, Shelley Guerra, showed incredible grace and patience during the writing along with candid criticism and helpful advice.

1 THE HOSPITAL

The room was 8 ft by 8 ft with an 8 ft ceiling. Each surface of the walls, the ceiling and floor was covered with dingy gray canvas mats. A single light bulb, set in the ceiling and protected by a steel grill, spilled harsh light into the cell 24 hours a day, ensuring that attendants could easily observe any activity of its occupant when looking through the protective glass window of the door, the only access to the room.

A thin, naked woman sat huddled in the far corner, her head between her drawn-up knees, her arms clinched tightly around her legs, swaying almost imperceptibly to a rhythm only she could hear. Her long black hair, once full and shiny, lay in limp, dirty strings across her hunched shoulders, her sides and thighs a pasty white with visible bones under the skin. Despair and fear seeped into the corridor, the only emissions from the soundproofed room. The woman was broken, without hope, and she was my mother.

I ran from the hospital, barely able to contain my tears of fear and rage. At fourteen, I thought I could handle anything. I had helped my father in his home construction projects since I was eight, added a morning and evening newspaper route for the *Wichita Falls Record News* at ten, and began working full time in the summers as a busboy in a popular restaurant at twelve. My earnings paid for clothes and entertainment, and my car, which I had purchased shortly after my birthday in January that year. I was 6 ft and weighed 170 pounds; I had survived street battles with boys as much as five years older, and I had some experience with drinking and sex. But I was not prepared to see my mother that day in those circumstances. I sat sobbing in my car, slamming my fists into the steering wheel, screaming curses at God, ashamed for myself and her, blaming the hospital for putting her misery and nudity on display, my Dad for not rescuing her, and myself for my failures as a son.

2 BEFORE THE STORM

Wichita Falls, my hometown, lies at the nexus of hot, moist air boiling up from the Gulf of Mexico and cold, dry winds sweeping down from Canada, the region of America meteorologists have dubbed "Tornado Alley". During late spring and early summer, the skies could instantly transform from puffy, white cumulus clouds drifting lazily to the horizon to boiling, black monsters spawning violent thunderstorms and devastating twisters. Neither a tornado's path nor its duration is predictable. Some touch the ground briefly, scattering dust and stripping leaves from trees before retreating into the angry cauldron of their birth. Others stay and visit, moving generally to the northeast and leaving broken trees, crushed buildings, and shattered lives in their path. Mother's mental illness was the tornado in our family, sometimes benign, more often raging, with lifetime impacts upon my father, my little brother and me.

In the 1950s, mental illness was still in the closet. Most people considered those with a mental disorder prone to unpredictable violence. As a result, psychotic incidents and the identity of those suffering from mental illness were kept secret within families, hoping to avoid the shame and stigma associated with being "crazy".

Mother suffered from manic-depression, a condition we now call Bipolar Disorder, cycling between periods of high energy, staying up all night, starting one project after another, eventually collapsing into deep melancholy and inactivity. She could appear normal for months, then spin off into a new cycle of frenzied animation. Her illness first appeared when she was in early 20s and I was in grade school. We never learned its cause, though her psychiatrist believed repressive memories of her early childhood were its roots. Whatever the reason, she and the rest of us went through periods of hell for more than a decade.

The eldest son, I was the first Lewis born in a hospital just at the close of World War II. My ancestors were hard-working, common people scrabbling out a living as small farmers in North Texas and Western Oklahoma. They worked six days a week, praised God on Sundays, and hoped to give their children a better life than they had.

When the Great Drought hit in the 30s, the winds blew, crops dried up, and the bankers took the farms, forcing my grandparents and their families to find new employment. As the Depression eviscerated the national economy, only part-time temporary work was available with four men applying for every job. Hard times forge resilient, serious people. Parents struggled to keep food on the table and clothes on the backs of their family members, taking any job available - when they weren't working, they were looking for work. Younger kids were left to fend on their own so long as they stayed out of trouble. Older kids, particularly males, were expected to add to the family income when they could.

PaPa, my Dad's father, was able to make a living from poker, dominos, and an occasional bout of bootlegging until he found work on the railroad as a nighttime engine tender, shoveling coal to feed the fires of steam engines during their idle hours. Grandpa Ross, my mother's Dad, worked as a foreman on a WPA crew building bridges and roads around North Texas before moving to the Promised Land in California. My grandmothers worked as hard as their husbands, tending gardens, taking in washing and ironing when it was available, sewing and mending family clothes, and picking cotton for extra money when the fields were ready.

Mom never talked about her early childhood, but Dad suspected that abuse of some sort had occurred which later resurfaced in her subconscious. A loner, she didn't participate in after-school activities, restricting her social life to neighborhood friends. The summer of her junior year in high school, she was a passenger in a deadly automobile accident in which two of her friends were killed. When she met Dad her senior year, she was eager to leave home, "to get away from the criticism of her mother" and start a new life.

Dad started working when he was 8 years-old, collecting discarded bottles and selling them to local bootleggers, delivering drugs for the town's only pharmacy, and joining his mother to pluck feathers on the killing floor of a local turkey processor. The pay was a nickel a bird — 2 to 3 carcasses was a good day's work.

Dad was diagnosed with tuberculosis when he was fourteen and sent to a sanatorium in Corpus Christi for a year. When he returned home to Childress, he and his family were shunned due to the fear of contagion, much like AIDs victims in the 1980s. The family moved to Wichita Falls for his senior year of high school to escape the social rejection of the smaller community.

As a TB victim, he couldn't serve in the Armed Forces, but he could work for the railroad, desperate for labor since most young men were being called up to fight. He and Mother eloped after their high school graduation and moved to Dallas where he began his new job. A year later, the Army called him for a medical exam. To everyone's surprise, the doctors discovered he had been misdiagnosed and was in perfect health. And with that, he was drafted and sent to Europe for the invasion of Germany.

When he returned home from the War, Dad rejoined the railroad. Lacking the seniority to bid the better routes, he worked whenever needed, on call day and night. Most routes were required several days away from home. He worked freight as well as passenger trains, the only difference being an impressive blue uniform and cap when he was scheduled on the latter. We lived in a small two-room apartment, a converted one-car garage, at the rear of my grandparents' house.

My grandmother, Nanny, was widowed in 1948 when my grandfather was killed in a head-on collision between two trains near Henrietta, Texas. PaPa was the engineer on one train and my father, in a horrible coincidence, a brakeman in the caboose of the second train. PaPa was scalded to death when the steam boiler burst; Dad's back broken when he was thrown from the colliding trains.

Nanny never remarried, a blessing for me and my brother upon whom she lavished love and attention during the dark days of my mother's illness. With a free train pass but only a meager pension, she found work as a school cafeteria cook where she toiled the next twenty years.

3 A SON IS BORN

Mother was nineteen when I was born, a slender coal-eyed beauty with mercurial moods, an omen of the problems to come in later years. She was extremely intelligent, intensely curious, and passionate in everything she attempted. Dad often teased her about how her eyes seemed to sizzle when she was angry, the rage leaking from her pupils as she struggled for control. When she thought she had been wronged, she would bow up and furiously attack the aggressor, unwilling to give even an inch until she had bloodied her foe.

Always a private person, she was never comfortable with other people, even babies. She had one or two friends from high school who lived across town, but visits required readying babies and two bothersome bus rides. As a consequence, Mom's days were generally spent sewing (she made all of our clothes) and reading when she wasn't tending to me.

Our living space was too small for a kitchen table and chairs so meals were prepared by Nanny and served in her house. Washing and ironing was split between the two of them, Nanny going to the public laundry at the end of the block for the washing and Mom doing the ironing for both families. She and Nanny, while friendly, were not social, separated by the generational divide between mother and daughter-in-law.

My father was more out-going, good-natured and loved by all of the kids of the neighborhood. On the days he didn't work, he actively participated in our games of cowboys and Indians (he was usually the first one killed), teaching the boys how to whittle, making rubber guns and stilts, and introducing us to "shinney", a hockey-like game played with a crushed can and broomsticks.

His standing in the neighborhood was almost mythical. Fitted with a body cast from his groin to his chest and wearing a loosely fitted shirt, he would nail tacks through his shirt and pants into the plaster surrounding his waist. Of course, the kids didn't know about his back or the cast, making my Dad the only guy in town who used nails, instead of a belt or suspenders, to keep his pants up.

In the summers, he would gather a group of the kids in the neighborhood and treat everyone to the public swimming pool; in winters after a snowfall, he would attach a wide, wooden sled to PaPa's car and drive slowly up and down the neighborhood streets, kids rushing from their houses to pile on and ride before tumbling off as others took their place.

Dad was a tall man for his generation, 6ft 2 inches, with ropey muscles that rippled in his shoulders and arms. Most times when he carried me, he would sweep me up to rest on his shoulders, so high that I towered over everyone and everything. At night, when he was home, he would sometimes lift me on the roof of our small house and climb up beside me. As we lay back, looking up at the stars, he told me stories of his childhood and life on the farm.

Like all couples, my parents had disagreements, mostly about money, which could quickly turn into arguments, and then to yelling. Dad usually retreated, knowing Mother would only escalate the rhetoric if he continued; he knew that words can hurt, stinging more sharply and leaving deeper scars than a physical attack. Arguments between the two of them most often ended with Dad slamming the only door to our little house and stalking through the neighborhood until he calmed down.

Mother encouraged my curiosity and indulged my interest in stories. Most Saturdays, she and I would ride the bus to the public library for the children's story time. She would check out five or six books and let me choose a couple of picture books to take home for the week. On many afternoons, we sat, side by side, on our couch, each reading from our own book. By the time I entered the first grade, I could read, having learned to spell words (with her help) from library books and the daily newspaper comics. When I turned five, Mother gave me my own library card, which allowed me to check out four books at a time. It was one of the best birthday presents I ever received.

Growing up the daughter of a tenant farmer, Mother had endured more than her share of slights, snubs, and bullies; she was determined that I would not be subjected to the same. She abhorred cravenness and expected me to face any terror, imagined or real, with immediacy and resolution. It was her, not my dad, who taught me to stand up for myself and to fight when necessary, despite the size or number of my adversaries.

"If you let a bully scare you, he'll take away everything you have," she said. "You might get beaten up once or twice before he decides to find an easier victim. But if you don't fight, he'll be on your back forever."

Whippings were a fact of life in my house and it never occurred to me that it was different for any other kid. Discipline wasn't something that my friends and I talked about. I tried my best to avoid making my parents angry, but if my behavior met with their disapproval, I learned to take my punishment, deserved or not, and move on. Trying to escape or hide inevitably resulted in a longer and harder chastisement.

In those days, Mother and Nanny were the disciplinarians, meting out "medicine" with switches cut from the backyard pecan or peach trees. "Spare the rod, spoil the child" was a common phrase in those days. And corporal punishment was simply like the sun rising in the morning or the cold coming in winter—you could pretty much count on it. If I got a whipping or a slap, I figured I probably deserved it whether I was guilty of any misdeed or not.

4 A BROTHER

In 1950, my brother, Randy, was born. That summer we moved into a rented two-bedroom house in a neighborhood across the town. The role of Big Brother came naturally to me and my parents were glad for me to have the responsibility. I changed diapers, rocked him to sleep, and fed him with bottles of mixed formula warmed in a saucepan of boiling water, always careful to squirt the heated milk on my bare forearm to ensure the liquid wasn't too hot.

In the afternoons and evenings, Mom would leave me in charge while she went to visit neighbors or play cards. When he cried, I comforted him. When he started walking, I crawled on my knees behind him to ensure he didn't fall and hit his head on the edge of a table or dresser. I loved him because he loved me. When I got a whipping, he cried for me; when I laughed, he would giggle, putting his little arms around my neck and hugging me so tight that it was sometimes hard to breathe.

My parents bought their first home when I was in the second grade, affordable because it badly needed repairs. When Dad wasn't working on the railroad, he was fixing up that old house. As far as I could tell, we were just like every other family in the neighborhood then – white, church going, with a father who worked in a blue-collar job and a mother who took care of the children and the home.

But sometime after that move, Mother changed, becoming moodier, more irritable, quicker to fly into a rage, and more apt to punish me. I got into trouble for everything - being too slow to come when called, breaking a water glass, forgetting to carry out the trash, or not taking care of my little brother. Whenever Randy cried, I usually cried too since Mother would blame me for failing to keep him happy and safe.

5 DISCIPLINE OR ABUSE

At some point, she forgot about switches, grabbing whatever belt, dog leash, kitchen spatula or spoon was close at hand. Sometimes her anger was so great, her disappointment and disgust with me so sudden, she would slap me across the face, leaving an imprint that could last an hour or more. In church, if I wiggled too much from boredom, she would pinch my forearm between her fingernails hard enough to draw blood. If I was too far to reach, she threw whatever was in her hand at me. As I grew older, these incidents became more frequent.

After each event, Mom would act as if nothing had happened, never explaining what I had done and never apologizing for anything she said or did. We would go for days, even weeks, at a time with no incident when suddenly, out of nowhere, she would explode with curses and strike me in her rage. She never hit Dad, who was often gone, or Randy, who was too small. I was the perfect whipping boy, big enough so that slaps and hits didn't cause black eyes or broken bones, but too small to avoid being the target.

I never knew what might set her off, but I grew unusually sensitive to the subtle clues when a blow-up was eminent and did my best to keep Randy and me out of her crosshairs. When I felt the tension build, I would take him to our bedroom, shut the door and stay as quiet as possible, only emerging when the outburst had passed. I consider this ability to read people a gift today, but back then, it was just how I weathered the storm.

The summer after I completed the fifth grade, I started my first paying job, throwing the morning and evening editions of the local newspaper. Work was natural for me as going to school or attending church on Sundays. A lesson passed from grandparent to parent to me, I learned that work is essential to life and everyone had to take responsibility for one's self.

At ten years old, I was one of the youngest paperboys in town. Back in those days, the daily newspaper was as important as the mail — customers expected it to arrive no matter the weather outside or if their paperboy was under the weather. And that makes running a newspaper route an inconvenience for everyone in the paperboy's family. If a customer is overlooked or the paper is torn or wet, someone has to make a second trip and deliver a replacement. You cannot have a paper route without family support. The daily inconvenience and everyday responsibility tests the resolve of every paperboy and most quickly find out the job is not for them.

Bundles of ten to fifty papers, each secured by a wire, were dropped by a route manager in the pre-dawn mornings and late afternoons at a drug store near my house. After removing the wire bindings around my bundles, I divided them between two large canvas bags that I slung over my shoulders and across my waist, a full bag resting against each hip. As I walked my route, I would retrieve a newspaper from one of the bags, fold it, and toss it on the porch of my customer. The faster I folded, the faster I could walk and finish the route. It usually took about an hour and a half to throw each edition.

My first route was over two miles long and included 100 customers on both sides of the streets; I earned a dollar a month per customer. With more money than I could spend, Mother helped me set up a savings account in the local bank. Even when I had full-time summer jobs, I continued to throw papers on one route or another until I graduated from high school. The money I made enabled me to buy my own clothes, pay for entertainment and dating when I was older as well as purchasing two old cars before I started college at 17.

Mother, though she didn't often say it, seemed proud of me. I loved reading and had an unusual memory so I made good grades without much effort, I had a well-paying job that enabled me to buy whatever toy or book we wanted without having to ask for money, I usually did my assigned chores without complaint, and I took care of my little brother. I was considered one of the better pitchers of my age group on the baseball teams I played on during the summers. Our newspaper included game reports and team standing for all Little League; I was in the sports headlines several times for no-hitters.

The best summer of my childhood was the year Dad coached our team, the Little Rascals. It was a good summer for Mother too; she went to all of the games, rooting for me as she stood behind the umpire and complained about his strike zone. Some days, she would hunker down in the driveway, squatting on her heels and wearing a big catcher's mitt for an hour or more, so I could practice my pitches. That summer was special because everyone seemed happy, Dad had time to spend with me and Randy and I generally was able to avoid doing anything to make Mother angry.

The last time she hit me was in the spring of my 6th grade, precipitated by a call from my elementary school principal, Miss Rollins. In my house, getting a call or a note from the school was never good news, often precipitating a whipping. My offense was using too much ketchup on the school meals, which set a bad example for other children, according to Miss Rollins. Unaware of the call or my principal's disapproval of my apparently gluttonous use of ketchup, I was completely caught off guard when Mother confronted me when I arrived home from school.

I was taller and heavier than her then, so her whippings were harmless. But on this occasion, as I turned away from her tirade hoping to get outdoors, she leapt on my back, locking her legs about my waist and wrapping her left arm around my neck. She began to punch me in the head with her fist.

I was too stunned to run, I just stood in the living room, being pummeled by my mother, letting her frenzy run its course. The punches didn't really hurt me, but I was crushed that my mother hit me with a closed fist. I understood discipline, but this was something different. This was pure unadulterated fury. I think that being so out of control scared her too, and she never hit me again.

A year later, when Dad attempted to spank me for mistakenly taking his work pants to the dry cleaners rather than the laundry as he instructed, he too realized that I had grown too much to be intimidated by a belt. Being too big to spank and knowing how I felt about my younger brother, Dad told me that Randy would get the punishment whenever I transgressed, knowing that the possibility was enough to keep me in line. It worked for a few years until I realized he would never follow through on his threat.

6 THE SKIES DARKEN

As the pendulum began to swing back the other direction, my mother's hot-tempered bursts were replaced by increasing bouts of depression, a condition even harder for me to understand. At the end of my 6th Grade term, she had started work with a local building contractor, leaving when Randy and I left for school and returning in the late afternoon.

Many evenings, she would go straight to bed from work, leaving Dad, if he was home, or me to fix dinner and clean the dishes. I didn't mind too much, the memories of her anger still fresh in my mind. Her self-imposed exile to the bedroom each evening meant I didn't have to walk on eggshells and could breathe easier. Randy and I would eat, clean up the dishes, and play in the neighborhood until it was time to go to bed.

On Saturday when she usually stayed in bed all day, we would fix a "King's Breakfast" for ourselves. Randy would set out plates and silverware, pour orange juice and milk, and butter bread for toasting in the oven while I fried bacon or ham and scrambled eggs in a big black cast-iron skillet, putting in the pre-buttered bread slices at the last minute for hot toast. We could fix whatever we wanted as long as we cleaned up and no one was the wiser.

Alarmed by her weight loss, Dad insisted that she go see our family doctor, and she finally relented. Bipolar disorder was not commonly recognized in those days, leading the doctor to diagnose her as simply "stressed". He suggested that she have a drink each night to relax. Unfortunately, one drink became two drinks, then three and more. Alcohol didn't help her mood, except to put her into a stupor each night. Dad never told me what was wrong, just that she was sick. Being the oldest, I was in charge when he was gone, making sure that she was sleeping each night before I went to bed.

Dad blamed himself for her sadness, presuming its cause was his failure to make enough money to have a big home or a nice car, enough money, or being away from home so much. His whole life revolved around Mother; he would have done anything to make her happy, no matter the cost in money or pain. Repairing the house transformed into a 3-year, full-blown remodeling project in an attempt to make her happy. He added a den and a covered concrete patio, redid the kitchen with new cabinets and appliances, replaced and painted the backyard fence. He and I jacked up our detached garage and moved it fifteen feet to create more room for his additions.

We didn't have any money, so Dad did all of the work himself, using me when I wasn't in school or one of his railroad friends when he could cajole them into helping him. He worked a regular trip on the railroad then, one and a half days gone and one and a half days at home. Before he left each trip, he would leave a list of projects that he expected me to complete while he was gone. This work was in addition to throwing my paper route, tending to Mother and Randy, and my regular chores. Nanny helped when she could, but most of the time, it was just Mother, Randy, and me.

It must have taken all my mother had in her to continue going out into the world every day to work. Presumably, she put on a happy face at the office, but when she came home, she retreated to the darkness and solace of her bedroom.

We stopped going to church and I stopped playing baseball. Sometime that year, it was apparent that Mother's problems were more than stress. Her doctor recommended a psychiatrist who prescribed barbiturates to break her alcohol habit. From my view, I couldn't tell the difference - she smelled better, but the drugs knocked her out even quicker than the drinks. She came home, sometimes fixed dinner, and then went to bed to read until the drug took effect.

She smoked so Dad constantly worried that she would fall asleep with a lit cigarette and set the bed on fire. It happened so frequently that the inside of her index and middle fingers were scarred from burning cigarettes after she passed out. When Dad was gone, my last chore at night was to check on her, stub out any cigarette, put away her book or magazine, and turn out the lights before I went to bed.

When Dad was home and I could shed my responsibilities, my friends and I wandered the dark streets of the neighborhood or gathered around a corner to smoke and tell stories about fights and girls. I knew neither of my parents approved of my friends or what we were doing, but no one appeared to notice as long as I was home by 10:30 PM.

Even drugs could not pull Mom from the depths of her depression. Dad continued his silence about her illness or treatment or when she might improve from Randy and me. I suspect he remembered his family's treatment in Childress when he came home from the sanatorium and didn't want Randy or me to experience any similar treatment because our Mother was crazy. Whatever his reasons, he never explained or ever said anything about Mother's condition. When he was home, I had to help with the work; when it was over, I escaped.

I was confused, scared, and angry with her and him. Mother had literally beat into me the belief that you never quit, you never stop trying, but she seemed to be giving up for no reason. She preached that I should never cry over spilt milk, to wipe it up and get on

19

about my business. Yet she lay around, feeling sorry for herself, while the rest of us struggled to keep the house clean, buy groceries, fix meals, and do all the necessary tasks to function every day. Even worse, Dad withdrew from the rest of us, spending his days working on his job or on the remodeling when he wasn't sequestered with Mom.

Abandoned and alone, I had no one to talk with except my little brother and a grandmother who was as much in the dark as the two of us. I wondered whether our lives would ever return to anything resembling normal, the kind of family routines of other kids in the neighborhood. And then, the inevitable happened. Mom overdosed.

Dad woke me late one night to help him get Mother from bed, semi-conscious, unable to stand. Under her doctor's orders, we walked and dragged her, Dad under one arm and me under the other, up and down the living room. She could barely put one leg in front to the other or mutter a coherent response to Dad's questions. From time to time, Dad would stop to call the doctor and report her progress while I propped her up as best I could. After three hours, we were told it was safe to return her to bed. Dad stayed with her while I got dressed, delivered my papers, and went to school.

We never talked about that night, leaving me to grapple for answers. Mother continued to retreat into her shell, shunning me, Randy, and Dad when we expected so little and would have accepted even less. I became increasingly resentful and rebellious, doing the minimum asked of me by Dad, and disobeying when I could get away with it.

7 SHOCK TREATMENTS

Over the next two years, Mother was hospitalized three times, the first two times for electroconvulsive therapy (ECT) and the last time for insulin coma therapy, collectively known as "shock treatments". Use of ECT to treat depression and schizophrenia became widespread in the United States during the 1940s and 1950s.

The treatment involves placing electrodes on each side of the head and delivering an electrical shock to the brain which causes the patient to have convulsions (what psychiatrists refer to as a "controlled seizure") lasting one to two minutes per treatment. Whether or not the patient feels pain is a matter of conjecture, since the patient either loses consciousness or is render unconscious by drugs before the treatment and does not remember the event. Most patients undergo a series of 8 to 10 treatments over a two-week period.

Dr. Peter Breggin, writing in the *Huffington Post* February 9, 2008, described the treatment as follows: "Shock treatment is simply closed-head injury caused by an overwhelming current of electricity sufficient to cause a grand mal seziure. When the patient becomes apathetic, the doctor writes in the hospital chart, 'No longer complaining.' When the patient displays the euphoria commonly associated with brain damage, the doctor writes, 'mood improved.' Meanwhile, the individual's brain and mind are so drastically injured that he or she is rendered unable to protest." Recent studies suggest that more than three-quarters of patients relapse after six months unless following a continuation of drug treatments.

Insulin coma therapy as a treatment for depression, popular in the 1940s and 1950s, had been discredited and discontinued in the United States by the 1970s. This treatment required injections of massive amounts of insulin sufficient to induce a coma for up to an hour. Treatments involved up to six comas a day, 6 days a week for a period or weeks or months. Sometimes, ECT was used in conjunction with the insulin treatment. Whether Mother received ECT with her insulin injections is not known since she couldn't remember the events and Dad didn't want to know the gruesome details.

Each time Mother went into the hospital, Randy and I were told that she needed to go into the hospital for "rest" which we interpreted to mean "get away from us". Randy and I weren't allowed to visit her in the hospital, presumably because of our age, but she would call from time to time to tell us she loved and missed us. Her calls to Dad were different; she would call and beg him to come get her, cursing him when he refused, and promising to leave him and us as soon as she was released.

Our only phone was on the wall next to the kitchen table. Dad would sit in the kitchen, smoking a cigarette, staring out the window into the night and listen to her berate and threaten him. From time to time, he would say, "Honey, I'm sorry I can't get you. Dr. Speakman says you need to stay." Afterwards he would hang up the phone and sit unmoving at the table, silent and alone with his thoughts.

Nanny sometimes moved in for the weeks when Mother was gone to fix meals since Dad practically lived at the hospital when he wasn't working. Mom would return from each hospitalization in good spirits, but subdued, as if she was with us, but her mind was somewhere else. She visited her psychiatrist every week and seemed to become brighter, more involved with us as the months passed. But the depression always returned, each time deeper than the episode before.

The costs of her treatments were more than Dad's health insurance would pay, so he resigned his position as the local Chapter President of the railroad union in order to take extra trips for more income, borrowed money from Grandpa Ross, and took a part-time job representing a ceramic tile company out of Dallas. When Mother tried to go back to work after her first hospitalization, she learned her old employer had replaced her while she was in the hospital. She found other office work, but it was temporary with poor pay. Fortunately, Randy and I weren't aware of the money problems; I had my paper route to cover the little money we needed to spend.

With Dad working around the clock and focused on Mother's recovery and my responsibility for Randy being met by Nanny, I was pretty much on my own by the end of the 7th grade. I had money, time and little supervision. I was at loose ends, not knowing where I fit in, and betrayed by Mother and Dad who seemed not to care what I did or who I was with. I would come home drunk or bloody and no one noticed. Grades were easy and the teachers usually liked me because I was smart, but I had a hard time making friends with my classmates.

By Junior High, most of my old friends from the neighborhood had either dropped out of school completely or were attending just to get to the age where they could drop out. I found myself caught between two very different worlds unable to make a choice: the highroad with the good guys or the alleys with the thugs. I spent the evenings stealing hubcaps and getting drunk, going to school, throwing papers and working at odd jobs when I could find them during the day. I just drifted along, not sure where I fit or if life would ever be different.

Lucky for me, Mother and Dad had done a good job in my early years establishing values, a work ethic, and responsibility. I believed, despite the whippings and the neglect, that they thought I was smart and could become a doctor, a lawyer, somebody who could work with their brains, not their brawn. But I was so angry and full of disappointment, wanting them to hurt as they hurt me, that the rebel, outlaw aspect of the hoodlum culture attracted me. So I teetered in the middle, being a good student during the day while drinking, fighting, and partying at night.

8. THE HOSPITAL AGAIN

Mom had been admitted to the hospital again. Even though Dad had forbidden me to visit her with the same old reason that I was too young, I had a driver license and a car. I needed to see her and I was sure she would be happy to see me. I stopped in the gift shop, bought a $3 bouquet of roses, and headed up the elevator to the 6th floor Psychiatric Unit. On the wall just past the elevators, there was a small blackboard listing each patient's last name and their room number.

As I strolled down the corridor, bouquet in my hand, searching for Mom's room, I glanced in the open doors seeing other patients and their families. It was like other hospitals I had visited - in some rooms, people were awake, happily talking with each other, while in others, the patients slept. My last thought before reaching her room at the end of the corridor was, "I hope I don't have to wake her up."

I don't know what happened to the flowers I carried that day. I don't remember where I went when I returned to my car. I never told Dad I disobeyed him and I couldn't bear to ever tell Mother that I had seen her so helpless, forlorn and full of despair. I didn't speak about that day for almost four years until I saw a psychiatrist my freshman year in college. The picture of her, so forlorn, so full of despair, is just as vivid today as that moment more than fifty years ago.

9 THE AFTERMATH

Mother began to improve following that last hospital admission, probably because of her weekly psychotherapy sessions for the next five years or possibly because she could no longer endure the punishment of shock treatments. Though Mom continued to cycle between normalcy and depression for another decade, their duration and intensity lessened over time. She only made one more suicide attempt.

While she improved, the relationship between Dad and me grew cool, even hostile at times as I struggled with my own identity. I had a difficult time making friends, afraid to trust people because I felt that they might disappoint me when I needed them most. With my jobs, I had plenty of money and I had grown used to making my own decisions and going where I wanted. I was bigger than most of my male classmates and neighborhood boys even though I was two and three years younger. My size, explosive anger, and unwillingness to back down from a fight protected me from bullies, but isolated me from the other students.

Dad had never liked football, probably because TB had robbed him of his chance to play. And football for a young man in Texas has always been the key to social acceptance and popularity. I desperately wanted to play, seeing the team as a way of getting the acceptance I sought so deeply. I had tried to play in Junior High school, but Dad only consented as long as I kept my paper route. I went through Spring training, leaving practice in the middle to throw papers and returning when I was done, but it was too much trouble and resented by the other players so I quit.

When I went to high school, my junior high coach, having been promoted to the high school football staff, called Dad and asked him to let me play. Dad refused, believing that the responsibility of a job was a more important lesson than playing a high school sport. That decision, unbeknownst to him, reverberated throughout my high school years. I was the biggest boy in my class and didn't play football. Why? I believed the other boys thought it was because I was afraid of being hurt, that I was a "sissy" or worse. As a consequence, I knew that I could never back down from a challenge, since doing so would only confirm my cowardice.

Every football weekend during my sophomore year in high school, I would join other boys, social outcasts equally at loose ends, to meet our counterparts from other schools to fight under the bleachers or behind the end zones, coming together in a frenzy of fists and kicks until scattering when the police would show up. If I couldn't show my courage on the football field, I could prove I was unafraid of being hurt in other ways.

I began boxing in the local Golden Gloves and other boxing tournaments in the towns around North Texas my junior year, a legally acceptable way of proving my manhood, but an activity no more likely to lead to popularity than street fighting.

Dad and I butted heads continuously during my high school years. I was too big to discipline and self-sufficient financially, thanks to his decision that I should work. Grades were just as easy as before - I became a member of the National Honor Society my junior year - and I avoided doing anything that would be considered criminal or might lead to arrest. But I rebelled openly, arguing over his slightest request, and generally became a pain in his ass.

Throughout high school, Dad spent most of his time worrying about Mother and trying to make life better for us. Neither he nor

Mom ever wavered in their determination that I would attend college, the first of my family to do so. I didn't realize it at the time, but their determination was to become my salvation.

The summer after my high school graduation, Dad bought 100 acres outside of town and started building a new home for us. I had a construction job putting in a telephone line between Paducah and Quanah, Texas for the summer, leaving every Monday morning at 6:00 AM and returning Friday evening. On Saturdays and Sundays, I would work with him on the new place, painting, building corrals and fences, and whatever else needed doing. Surprisingly, that was probably the first work I didn't resent, knowing that I would be leaving for college in the fall, never to return for anything more than a visit.

One Saturday afternoon after we finished framing the second floor of the house, Dad left and returned with a six-pack of beer for us to share, a sign he recognized me as a man even though I was only seventeen. As we lay on the floor looking up through the unfinished beams of the roof, we started talking as we had years before on the roof of the little house that had been a garage.

"You've done a really good job this summer. I don't know how I'm going to get all of this done when you're gone," he said.

"Randy's big enough to help. He's older than I was when you started on the old house," I said.

"Well, it's different for him. He doesn't piss me off or argue with me like you did, but he's always got an excuse for not being able to help," Dad replied, laughing. "Besides, I don't want to make the same mistakes with him that I did with you.""What do you mean? What mistakes did you make with me?"

"I put an awful lot on you when you were young. You had responsibilities that most kids your age never had, particularly with your mother. I look back and wish things had been different, but it's too late now." He took a drink of beer. "You don't know it now,

28

but someday you'll realize how hard it is to be a father and have to make choices about the people you love. Sometimes, even with the best intentions, you make the wrong choice and you and the people around you have to live with your mistake."

"You did a pretty good job. I'm going to Texas in a month and I'm sure I'll make good grades and graduate on time."

"I'm not worried about you, Mick. You're smart, you're not afraid of hard work, and you take responsibility. I just wish I had spent more time with you growing up and that we knew each other better."

"You did all right and you had Mom to take care of then. The only thing, I wished you had let me play football." I grinned. "I could have been a monster on the field, better than baseball."

"Your Mom did need me then and now and I've always given her all that I had to give. I should have spent more time with you and Randy, though, but I knew you could handle it and take care of him and I didn't know if your mother would make it." He took a long drag from his cigarette and tossed the butt over the edge of house. "We'd better get going. Don't you have a date tonight?"

We gathered the tools and drove back to town, those few minutes of clicking together without rancor, blame, or excuses treasured in our respective memories for all time.

During Christmas vacation of my college freshman year six months later, Mother slit her wrists before being discovered by my brother, then 12 years old, and taken to the hospital by my father. What triggered the event is uncertain, but the episode, in hindsight, represented the last throes of the storm before the sun finally broke through and we at last began to restore the bonds of family.

10 REDEMPTION

The two of us sat on the porch of his beach home, old men and the only survivors of those times fifty years before. Our careers over or ending, with grown children and grandchildren, we remain as close as when we huddled together behind the closed bedroom door waiting for the storm to pass.

"Do you ever think of those days now?" I asked. Mother had passed almost fifteen years before and Dad has been gone a decade.

"Sure, more now than I ever did then. I only have happy memories. I was too young to know what was going on with Mother and too little to care. Besides, I always had you taking care of me," answered my brother.

"I must have done a pretty good job, considering all of this," I laughed, gesturing at the multi-floored house, the expanse of beach, and the distant Chicago skyline across Lake Michigan. "The folks were really proud of what you accomplished, the man you've become."

"They were proud of you too, Mick, they just didn't know how to show it. And they worried about you, Mom especially. You were always taking risks, even though you had a great family and more money than you would ever need."

"I wish we had do-overs in life, for their sake and mine. I wasted years blaming them for my rage and insecurities before understanding that people do the best they can in the circumstances they find themselves." I lit another cigarette and leaned back in my chair.

After a moment, Randy replied, "I know it wasn't easy for you; it wasn't fair to have to take care of me or to feel alone and unloved. No kid should ever have to go through that. But it wasn't anyone's fault. Mother was sick, there was no one else to care for her except Dad, and he knew you were strong enough to take care of me and help him when you had to. It was a shitty situation for the three of you, but you survived and made it through."

I nodded, unwilling to speak as the old memories of loneliness and inadequacy flooded me. I knew that Dad had wasted two decades blaming himself for Mom's troubles, sure that his inadequacies were the root of her unhappiness. She was everything to him, but what he gave never seemed to be enough. He sacrificed time with his sons, atoning for deficiencies that didn't exist, never realizing that those years would be lost, never to be recaptured. We were strangers for a long time; it took me decades to forgive him for keeping me at arms' length. But he never forgave himself. His last words to Randy and me, as he lay on his deathbed, were "I'm sorry."

"I think Mother loved you most of all because she saw so much of herself in you. The passion, the grit, the unwillingness to bend, no matter the cost. You dream like she did and I've seen the same rage and fury overcome you that plagued her. She believed you understood her better than anyone. The real tragedy is that she never became the mother she and you wanted her to be, always understanding, never critical, eternally loving." Randy stopped talking as we watched the sun set on the horizon, each of us remembering those childhood days.

"Mom, I think, finally made peace with her devils, accepting the past and determined to be a good grandmother. And she was, to your kids and mine. Mick, we were lucky to have parents who loved us and did the best they could with the hands they were dealt."

As the sun set and the darkness closed around us, I reached across to squeeze his hand, memories of those days racing through my mind. The pain has gradually receded, replaced by a sorrow of the loss of what might have been, but never happened. I'm finally at peace and comforted by the many blessings of a family inextricably bound together by hardship, tragedy, and triumph more deeply than blood, genes, or ancestors could ever fashion.

ABOUT THE AUTHOR

Michael R Lewis has dug ditches and washed dishes for minimum wage, sold shoes and tax shelters, advised people how to make and spend a fortune, partied with rock stars, and studied to become an Episcopal priest. He has made and lost millions of dollars in industries ranging from oil and gas exploration to wood treating. He was a Principal in a National Management Consulting firm, a Senior Executive with the largest multi-state not-for-profit health insurer in the United States, an Executive gun for hire, and started companies in numerous industries before retiring in 2012 at age 67.

Over the past two years, he has contributed more than 200 articles on investments, business management, entrepreneurship, and the economy to publications and websites including MoneyCrashers.com, *Forbes*, *Huffington Post*, and National Mortgage Professional.com. "The Storm" is his first published book to be followed by a second titled "One Step at a Time: How to Get What You Want From Life" in the summer of 2014. His personal website and blog are at MichaelRLewis.org

www.ingramcontent.com/pod-product-compliance
Lightning Source LLC
Chambersburg PA
CBHW060703280326
41933CB00012B/2286

ISBN: 978-0-88493-016-7

THE FIELD AND IMPORTANCE OF POLITICAL ECONOMY

and

THE PAYMENT OF LABOR

by Albert S. Bolles

This book contains Chapters I and II of
"Chapters in Political Economy" by
Albert S. Bolles. The original book
published in 1874 contained 16 chapters.
It is being republished as 6 separate
books by William R. Parks.

William R. Parks
WParksPublishing@aol.com

www.wrparks.com

PREFACE.

The chapters embraced in this work treat of the leading economic questions which are rife in our country. Although most of the chapters have appeared in magazines during the past two years, yet a unity will be found pervading the work. An attempt has been made to handle the questions in a thorough manner, to dig down for principles which are fundamental, though the author was conscious that, in so doing, the work would lose something of its interest to those who only seek to glide over the surface of things. If ever the questions of labor, money, exchange, taxation, and the like, are to receive a permanent settlement, they must be traced back into the region where prejudice and feeling do not enter, however dry and uninviting may be the investigation.

Norwich, Conn., September, 1874.

Note: This book contains Chapters I and II. The original book contained 16 chapters listed below. It is being republished as 6 separate books. Order the books from Amazon.com by searching on the chapter titles.

CHAPTERS

I.

THE FIELD AND IMPORTANCE
OF POLITICAL ECONOMY.

In *The Principles of Economical Philosophy*,* MACLEOD has given an elaborate criticism upon several definitions of political economy, and then offered one himself which, in his opinion, "appears to state clearly and distinctly the nature and extent of the science, and to be free from the ambiguities connected with the words wealth and value." At the risk of being ambiguous, we shall not give a definition so precise, because a commoner one can be more easily understood. According to an old and well-received definition, the principles of political economy relate to the production, distribution, exchange, and consumption of wealth. No higher origin is claimed for these principles than an enlightened self-interest. They are such as every man entertains having regard solely for his own interests from the most enlightened point of view.

Although without moral foundation, these principles yield the same results in the production, distribution, exchange, and consumption of wealth, as obedience to a perfect moral code. Wherever economic and moral science touch, the principles of human

* P. 122, 2d ed.

conduct prescribed by each are seen to be the same.* The remark of Dr. WAYLAND is perfectly true, that "the principles of political economy are so clearly analogous to those of moral philosophy, that almost every question in the one may be argued on grounds belonging to the other."†

For example, moral science condemns laws made in restraint of trade. ‡ It teaches that every man has the right to traffic where he pleases, unfettered by State lines. The primary object of enacting such laws is to enrich the few at the expense of the many. The protectionist urges their enactment for the public good, or for some reason beyond his own aggrandizement; the history of legislation clearly shows that the prime object of all protective laws is to benefit particular individuals, or a class, and not all. Of course, moral science condemns such legislation.

They are condemned by political economy also, which looks at them with the sharp eye of enlightened selfishness. It sees that if the public good is the object of protection, everything must be protected conducive to that end; and if this doctrine be admitted, protective laws will be enacted so generally as to afford protection to nothing. If the principle is not to receive a logical and just application, and merely that a few things most needed by the public are to be protected, their increased cost to the consumer will result in his protecting himself by charging more for whatever he sells, so that, after a time, the effect of protective laws is completely neutralized.

Moral science, then, condemns legal protection because it is wrong; economic science because it is impossible to get protection by operation of law. The conduct of people in either case is the

---

* PERRY's *El. of Polit. Econ.*, p. 37, 5th ed.
† Pref. *El. of Polit. Econ.*, p. 4, 4th ed.
‡ For an elucidation of the operation of protective laws, see chap. 15th.

same, only it is impelled by different motives in one case than in the other.

As this position will hardly be assailed by any one—that the principles of economic and moral science yield the same results— is it not better to transfer the principles of political economy from a selfish to a moral basis? We favor this transfer for four reasons.

First, more persons will be drawn to the study of economic principles. Now, it is said, they are cold and bloodless, and tend to increase human selfishness. If made a portion of the truths of moral science, this objection to them will disappear.

Secondly, in the classification of knowledge, it will be easier to find an appropriate place for political economy. Instead of being a piece of knowledge standing apart by itself, it will form a subdivision of moral science. Political economy in that case would constitute that part of moral scienee relating to the production, distribution, exchange, and consumption of wealth.

Thirdly, after deriving the principles from a moral source, they can be enforced by showing their harmony with enlightened self-interest. Thus the combined power of morality and selfishness can be used to sustain these principles by founding them upon a moral basis. We have previously seen in the example of protective legislation, how the selfish mind, cold, clear, and enlightened, supplements and enforces the transparent conclusions of morality. Moral science condemns such laws because they are wrong; economic science because they are at war with self-interest and have only a nominal, and not a real, existence after a period.*

Fourthly, political economy is properly a subdivision of moral science, because the will operates in every transaction, with which

* The insufficiency of enlightened self-interest as a competent basis for economic science has been ably discussed by FREDERIC HARRISON in the *Fort. Rev.*, vol. i, p. 356.

economic science is concerned. This faculty exercises only moral functions. If the principles of political economy were immutable, if the will were a stranger in their production, if no moral quality adhered to them, political economy would be entitled to a seat among the exact sciences. But these principles are not fixed, because the human will is an element determining what they are. The rules which have guided men in the past respecting the acquisition or disposition of their wealth, are only hypotheses in respect to what they will do in the future. Quite absurd is the claim that economic principles are absolutely fixed, and therefore purely scientific principles. Having no place in exact literature, and the will being a part of the machinery by which economic principles are created, they ought to be relegated to the domain of moral science.*

If the principles of political economy are transferred from a selfish to a moral basis, the method of searching for them is not changed. Economic principles are still the fruit of induction. And it is worthy of note how extensively employed is the inductive method in political economy. ADAM SMITH, it is true, did not write an inductive treatise. His *Wealth of Nations* is a great landmark in the history of thought, but its success is due to the fact that he put ten years of patient labor upon the work, combining in the happiest manner a philosophic insight with a knowledge of practical life, deducing therefrom principles which have found universal acceptance. It is easier to dream and speculate than to burrow amid a great mass of facts; yet, as the gold in the

---

* JEVONS, in his *Theory of Polit. Econ.*, has united moral and economic science, making pleasure the end, and declaring that "the object of economy is to maximise happiness by purchasing pleasure, as it were, at the lowest cost of pain" (p. 27). As JEVONS is a utilitarian, of course pleasure is the highest end for man according to his philosophy, though he gives a wider interpretation to the term than his master, BENTHAM, whom he so much admires. See pp. 27-32.

earth can be found only by toilsome mining, so the gold of economic truth is hid in great masses of facts which must be dug over to find it. Never did finer logicians or acuter reasoners exist than the schoolmen; never did a class of men commit greater mistakes. These followed from wrong premises. Political economy has followed too much a similar method. This is one reason why it has failed to convert men. It has been too speculative.* The change of method among economists in this respect is remarkable. Fifty years since, THOMAS TOOKE applied the inductive method in his *History of Prices* with enduring success. Later, RICHARD JONES applied it to the subject of Rent ; similarly, EDWIN CHADWICK in his investigations into the questions of Factory and Infantile Labor, and Sanitary and Poor-Law Legislation. In 1867, ROGERS published his work upon the *Agricultural Prices and Wages in England during the Twelfth and Thirteenth Centuries,* a monument of patient investigation, a work which gave a new rendering of the social and economic history of ENGLAND for the period it covered, "enabling us to see," says NEWMARCH,† "in detail, how far-reaching and potent were wages, prices, and pestilences in modifying from top to bottom the coherence of the English polity, and the power of our sovereign lord the king, under the early Plantagenets."

Other economic works might be spoken of, prepared in a similar way, DUDLEY BAXTER's books upon *National Income,* and *Taxation of the United Kingdom,* and LEONI LEVI'S *History of British Commerce,* are examples. As for FRANCE, she has been noted for her economists who have burrowed and lived among the facts.

* "Half, and more than half, of the fallacies into which persons who have handled this subject have fallen, are the direct outcome of purely abstract speculation." ROGERS in preface to his edition of *Smith's Wealth of Nations,* p. 41.

† Address before the British Social Science Association, 1871.

CHEVALIER, in all his works, has kept close to the inductive method. So has M. DE LAVERGNE when treating upon the moral economy of his own and other countries. M. LEVASSEUR and M. LE PLAY have considered the claims of the working classes of FRANCE in a similar manner. The same may be said of M. JULES SIMON.

Of the political economists in our own country following this method, not so much can be said. The most prominent example who has addressed himself to the mastery of facts as the foundation of his subsequent reasonings, is DAVID A. WELLS. In his reports to the National Government and to the State of NEW YORK, and in other papers, he has adhered rigidly to the inductive method. For many years pursuing physical science, he has employed its methods in finding out the principles of political economy. His results have, in some instances, been as unexpected to himself as they were startling to the public. They are none the less true, however, or less likely of being accepted in the end. The National and State Governments are learning the value of this method, for they are appointing commissions and requiring investigation and reports upon many subjects lying in the province of political economy. · Never was a more inviting field of investigation open to the student of economic science than our own country, nor one where patient, honest investigation was more needed. The facts are lying around in the greatest profusion, while the honest and accurate gatherers are few. ·

Although the true principles of political economy are ascertained by induction, and all others are only guessed, yet none are hard, fixed laws that never change in their occurrence, like the movements of the sun. On the other hand, the element of human freedom, as we have previously remarked, enters into their composition, preventing us from determining their absolute truth, as we can the laws of physical science. MACLEOD, in his *Principles of Economical Philosophy*,* has labored industriously, and with great ability, to bring economic science within the domain of physical science, but we cannot regard his attempt as successful. COMTE and JOHN STUART MILL have comprehended the nature of economic principles more perfectly. They admit the play of the human will; hence the Frenchman was consistent in rejecting political economy from his scheme of positive philosophy. One of his disciples,† in vindicating his master, has very well said: "So far as physical conditions go, and up to a point where moral conditions begin, strict scientific laws can be established. . . . Directly the data of the study become affected by moral conditions, the conclusions of the economist as such cease to be scientific laws, and are only hypotheses." For this reason, therefore, political economy can never become an exact science. However far we may carry our inductions, a large element of variation must be allowed for the action of the will. As the land surveyor can never determine with exactness surface and direction on account of variation of the needle, so the economist can never discover by the most patient study of facts, any unalterable laws of economic science, because of the infinite variations in the will of men. The farthest he can go is to ascertain how men have acted under former conditions, and form the hypothesis that, under like conditions, similar actions will be produced.‡

As the principles of political economy are ascertained by induc-

---

* Chap. I. † FREDERIC HARRISON, *Fort. Review*, vol. 1, p. 369.

‡ DAVID SYME has declared that the "inductive method is alone applicable to the investigation of economic science, and that we shall never be able to make any solid progress so long as we continue to follow the A PRIORI method." *West. Rev.*, vol. 95, p. 100. On same subject, see Prof. CAIRNES' *Character and Logical Method of Polit. Econ.*, Lec. II.

tion, any one capable of making an induction can find them out. A knowledge of economic principles involved in a particular pursuit is not necessarily limited to those engaged in that business. The sole advantage one man has over another of equal ability is in a knowledge of facts, out of which inductions spring.

Thus the charge, that only business men, practical men, can understand the principles of political economy, is •conclusively refuted. The charge contains this basis of truth and no more— that business men often know more facts concerning their business than outsiders; hence they are more capable of forming correct conclusions.

The history of political economy attests the truth of this assertion. For, who are the most successful cultivators of the science? Who have wrought out those principles which most persons are willing to admit as true and of great importance? Are they the discovery of practical men? By no means. The great lights in economic science, from the day of ADAM SMITH to this, have not been practical men.* Political economists have walked with the man of business, have gleaned from him all that he knew, and, not content with exhausting one storehouse of experience, have exhausted others, dug in rare and rich mines of which practical men had no knowledge perhaps, or no time or inclination to explore. As the reader of the description of a battle may acquire a more perfect knowledge of it than a participator therein, because, as an eye-witness, the latter knows only what happened immediately around him, so the political economist may acquire a wider knowledge of economic principles governing a particular business

* "In every country in which it has been successfully cultivated, most of the contributions to it of any value have been made by writers who were not of the business world, but surveyed its operations from a distance; men for whose opinions on business matters few merchants or manufacturers would have given five cents." *The Nation*, vol. 2, p. 146.

even, than a person who has given to it the attention of a life-time.

A political economist can see economic principles more clearly because his view is not mystified by pecuniary interest. His judgments are unclouded by prejudice; undisturbed by the thought of gain or loss. We need not indulge in any platitudes as to the unconscious warpings of opinions and beliefs by interest and desire; the fact is common to all.

A conspicuous illustration of the eminent service sometimes rendered by the theoretical economist, is the creation of the National banking system. This was the work of the Rev. JOHN McVICKAR, Professor of Political Economy in Columbia College. In 1827, he wrote a letter to a member of the legislature of the State of NEW YORK, entitled *Hints on Banking*, in which he developed the system now in practice. This discovery excited the admiration of an eminent banker, JOHN E. WILLIAMS, President of the METROPOLITAN BANK of New York, who has remarked that " to a practical man of business—an every-day banker—it seems wonderful that a scholar, investigating questions in political economy, on purely scientific principles, should be able to see not only the practical workings of existing laws, and understand the indissoluble relations of money and trade, but should be also able to foresee and foretell what changes were necessary to produce the highest prosperity and secure the greatest safety to the community." *

Not infrequently the principles of political economy are declared to be mere theories. Some of them are nothing more. The difference, however, between theoretical principles, and those derived from experience, is clear enough. Scientists are continually mistaking principles for theories, regarding things as proved which are

* *Old and New Mag.*, vol. 8, p. 590.

not, but only asserted or believed.   That theories are useless, as some contend, we deny.   Nay, they are absolutely necessary ; no man can conduct his business without them.   " What is practice without theory," enquires an eminent French economist,* " but the employment of means without knowing how or why they act." To which the words of Prof. PRICE† may be added.   " It is a mistake, though a very common one, to suppose that practical men, as they are called, are destitute of theory.   The exact reverse of this statement is true.   Practical men swarm with theories, none more so."   Theories are well enough,‡ only they must be regarded as such ; no harm is done to economic science in including both, if the separation of principle from theory be clearly made.

The flaw with some of the principles of political economy, like many of the inductions of science, is that they rest upon insufficient foundations.   A few facts are gathered, and from them a principle is deduced, which, indeed, may be correct, yet which would give way to another principle, perhaps, were a wider induction made.   Every result is produced by several causes, nevertheless we are constantly blundering by satisfying ourselves with finding a single cause, and so look no farther.

To some it may seem a waste of time and space to say anything concerning the importance of knowing the principles of political economy.   Yet there are peculiar reasons for saying something on this point.   The extraordinary prosperity that has visited our country has spread a kind of poetic haze over the whole machinery of society, and led us to regard all inquiry into its

---

* SAY. *Treat. on Polit. Econ.*, Intro., p. 24, 4th Am. ed. † *Princ. of Currency*, p. 1.

‡ Sir WILLIAM HAMILTON says: "Theory is dependent on practice: practice must have preceded theory; for theory being a generalization of the principles on which practice proceeds, these must originally have been taken out of, or abstracted from, practice." *Lecture on Met.*, p. 120, Am. ed.

working as an idle speculation. Before the enactment of the great tragedy between the North and South, there were but few questions relating to the administration of the government involving the application of any principles of political economy. The great debates in Congress were upon constitutional law, internal improvements, slavery, and like questions. With the breaking out of war, these questions passed away. The country had gone through the formative period of finding out the meaning and scope of the organic law. Congress was confronted with economic questions. With these it was ill prepared to deal. It had only the scantiest knowledge of them, except the question of taxing importations. The *Congressional Globe* is the enduring monument of the ignorance displayed by members of congress upon questions involving economic principles.*

To what new economic conditions did the war give rise? It created a great debt, the interest and principal of which must be provided for and paid. A national currency and system of banking have been created. How our country blundered in raising money to maintain the war, and spent it; how the strife might have been carried on and the debt been less than half it is, are mistakes which we shall not recall.

Unquestionably our country has suffered most fearfully from an ignorance of, or failure to apply, some of the most familiar principles of political economy. One of its most distinguished teachers,

* We shall give a couple of fair specimens. "All governments fix the value of gold and silver; and without their government stamp gold and silver would be a simple commodity, like other things having intrinsic value. Some governments fix the value of coin higher, and some lower; just as each for itself chooses to determine."—E. G. SPAULDING; *speech on Demand-Note Bill, January* 28, 1862.

"This currency," referring to demand notes or legal tenders, "can be converted in such a manner as to yield six per cent. interest on its par value; it can never greatly depreciate, because the moment the capitalist holding it sees any evidence of its depreciation, he will convert it into the bonds bearing interest, giving him a permanent income. Thus it secures itself against over-circulation."—*Speech of* SAMUEL HOOPER *on same subject.*

AMASA WALKER, clearly set forth in a congressional speech, during the early part of the war, how it might be carried on at less than half the expense which Congress was likely to incur, by sticking to specie payments, instead of abandoning them for an irredeemable paper currency. His words, deemed foolish then, have long since borne evidence of their wisdom and truth. The issue of an irredeemable currency, so pointedly condemned by him and other economists, has wrought a thousand curses to our country, from which we are suffering to-day and are to suffer for years to come.

Letting the past go, many of our politicians do not yet understand the principles of political economy, the application of which are needed to settle questions confronting the nation. For example, there are questions of taxation both upon imports and property at home. The principles which should govern in these matters, some of our politicians are as ignorant of as the grandest truths in astronomy. The National banking system, the currency, free banking, specie payments, redemption of legal-tender notes— are all subjects within the domain of political economy, whose principles must be mastered if these matters are to receive a rational settlement. The views entertained upon these questions, the nonsense and ignorance displayed by Congress when grappling with them, would be laughable were the results not so sad and so disastrous to the people.

Every session of Congress discloses its inability to grapple with economic questions.* When matters of foreign policy are discussed,

---

* Perhaps our congressmen may profit by learning what BURKE thought of political economy: "If I had not deemed it of some value, I should not have made political economy an object of my humble studies from my very early youth to near the end of my service in Parliament, even before (at least to any knowledge of mine) it had employed the thoughts of speculative men in other parts of EUROPE. At that time it was still in its infancy in ENGLAND, where, in the last century, it had its origin. Great and learned men thought my studies were not wholly

or treatment of the Indians, or internal improvements, or, in the olden time, when dealing with slavery, a knowledge and mastery of the several subjects is evinced, although not all reached similar conclusions. This cannot be said of the senators and representatives in Congress in respect to economic questions, excepting a member who appears occasionally, for a brief season, within the national halls.

It is desirable, therefore, for every person proposing to serve his country in a public capacity to understand the principles of political economy, for they apply to the most important questions of national legislation.* No one will dispute how the character of national legislation has been changed by the war, and that financial measures and taxation are the most conspicuous questions upon which Congress legislates.

Again, the principles of political economy are growing in importance to the individual in his business relations. Consider the relations of capital and labor. How this question looms up before the whole world. It is one of the mightiest questions of the age. It has assumed a magnitude surpassed by no other. It is convulsing the business of manufacturing and other pursuits. For years and years this question will hang like a mighty cloud over the people. Is it not desirable to find out all that can be known concerning the relation of the capitalist and laborer? Yet who has investigated this question most profoundly? The political economist. The question lies within the domain of economic

thrown away, and deigned to communicate with me now and then on some particulars of their immortal works. Something of these studies may appear incidentally in some of the earliest things I published. The House has been witness to their effect, and has profited of them, more or less, for above eight-and-twenty years."—*Letter to a Noble Lord on the attacks upon his pension;* BURKE's *works, vol.* 5, *p.* 192.

* Said COBDEN to the House of Commons, when addressing them on the corn laws: "It may be material for you to get right notions of political economy; questions of that kind will form a great part of the world's legislation for a long time to come."—*Speeches, vol.* 1, *p.* 384.

science. And it has been patiently and thoroughly investigated by the economist in all its phases.*

The same is true of other questions. Take the question of restrictive laws upon foreign importations, for example. Shall the policy of the government be continued? Is it for the advantage of any one; if so, whom? Are the laboring classes benefited by it? Is the National banking system a good one? Do we need more currency? These, and a host of similar questions, fall within the range of political economy, and have been more carefully investigated by economists than by empirics, who, possessing a little knowledge and having achieved fortunes, find it hard to believe that any one has anything to tell them upon trade, finance or commerce.†

For these special reasons, the principles of political economy have a value to the statesman and man of business hitherto unknown or denied.‡ It is gratifying to know that a knowledge of these principles is rapidly widening. The issuing of eleven editions of Prof. PERRY's *Elements of Political Economy* within so short a period, is proof that the people are awaking out of sleep and coming to believe that ignorance of the principles of political economy—which has cost us so much as a nation and as individuals—is not bliss pure and unalloyed. A little wisdom is to be preferred, and the streaks of light beginning to be seen in Congress we trust will grow in power and magnitude until that body possesses the knowledge necessary to discuss and settle wisely the great economic questions which involve the prosperity and happiness of the republic.

* If the remark of COBDEN be true—that "the principles of political economy have elevated the working class above the place they ever filled before"—should they not seek to master these principles?—*Speeches*, vol. 2, p. 373.

† The advantages to be derived by the Christian ministry from the study of political economy are admirably stated by Prof. BOARDMAN in the *Bib. Sacra*, vol. 23, p. 73.

‡ The reasons why political economy has not been cultivated in AMERICA, are concisely given in *The Nation*, vol. 2, p. 255.

II.

THE PAYMENT OF LABOR.

This question has attracted more attention in EUROPE, especially in ENGLAND, than here; for there laborers have been paid less and have suffered more, and they have oftener resorted to strikes and other rude methods to increase their wages. Yet the wave of discontent has reached our shore, and is breaking, with more or less fury, over every part of the land. Not a more important question in political economy calls for settlement; not one is likely to give rise to graver difficulties and greater suffering before a settlement is reached.

The contest between capitalist and laborer is a contest between present and accumulated labor. Capital is labor saved, nothing more.* The contest is between him who has saved his labor, or inherited it, and him who has less. It is a contest of the laborer with the laborer, after all.

There is a very gradual shading between the capitalist having many millions, and the laborer having nothing except his brains and limbs. One man has a vast fortune, another a hundred thousand dollars, another a quarter of that sum, another his farm, another his brains, one a store of goods, one a set of tools, another a shovel. Thus the gradations from the capitalist to the

---

* Technically, labor is exertion demanding something for itself in exchange.—PERRY, p. 122.

laborer shade off almost imperceptibly, and it is not easy to class-
ify all persons.

As to the true relation between capitalist and laborer, there is
scarce a division of opinion.   Says Prof. PERRY :* " There is no
sense or reason in the common jealousy of workmen towards employers.   There is no real antagonism between them.   Their
interests lie along the same line.   They are partners in the same
concern."   And this is the common language of all who have
investigated the subject.

It may be very easily shown that the true interests of labor and
capital are identical.   Without the employment of capital, laborers
in many cases could not live.   An accumulation of capital is
necessary to undertake most of the enterprises of the world.
While a machine is being made, a railroad built, a crop raised,
capital is required upon which to subsist.   Without capital, people
would live from hand to mouth, according to the common saying;
that is, would return to their original state, and live by fishing,
hunting, the fruits of the earth, and the like.   It is by saving,
accumulating capital, that the world has been able to make such
progress—to build factories and railroads, and undertake thousands
of enterprises, the returns upon which, though sure to come, may
be long delayed.

The capitalist has the means to accomplish these things, if
united with labor.   He can do nothing without it.   To build a
railroad, labor is just as essential as capital.   Both are indispensa-
ble elements.   Hence the theoretical truth that they operate in
perfect harmony.   Were the rich man totally unable to unite his
capital with labor, he would become a beggar ; were the workman unable to get employment from the capitalist, he would

* *El. of Polit. Econ.*, p. 148, 5th ed.

starve. The interests of the two are, therefore, inseparably united; their need of each other is equally great.

What is their actual position? This is not a pleasant investigation to make. We shall present a dark picture of the motives ruling the greatest portion of mankind. Yet let it be remembered, that our investigation is general; it does not apply to every individual case. There are unselfish employers and laborers. We seek to analyze the motives which generally actuate the two classes. What are these?

The laborer is determined to get the highest wages for the least work; the employer the most work for the least wages;* The motives of the two classes are the same. The question of paying or receiving a reasonable compensation is not the one determining the question. How much can I get? how little can I pay? these are the questions asked.

The trades-unions of GREAT BRITAIN have declared this again and again. In the *Edinburgh Review*,† their object is clearly set forth: "'The final end' of the trades-unions is 'to raise to the highest practical point the rate of wages,' and it is their maxim that no work should be done heartily; to 'evade' work and to 'loiter' at work are rules; 'he who is most skillful in these arts is the greatest benefactor to his order;' 'the sluggard, according to the standard of the unions, must be the model workman;' the unionists have plans for making work that is useless to their employers; they, in some cases, oppose the use of machinery, and compel the public to make use of inferior articles—for example, hand-

---

* BURKE has said: "There is an implied contract, much stronger than any instrument or article of agreement, between the laborer in any occupation and his employer—that the labor, so far as that labor is concerned, shall be sufficient to pay to the employer a profit on his capital and a compensation for his risk; in a word, that the labor shall produce an advantage equal to the payment."—*Thoughts and Details on Scarcity*, vol. 5, p. 137.

† July No., 1868.

made bricks: the Leeds bricklayers have a rule against one man carrying more at a time than 'the ridiculously small number of eight bricks'; walking slowly to work, so as to consume as much as possible of the master's time, has been acted on as a rule; the trades-unions aim at 'making as much work as possible,' 'by rendering the labor of each less efficient;' the union is, in some cases, so 'omnipotent over masters,' that 'the industrial machine is turned topsy-turvy;' in cases of outrage, employers are afraid to prosecute, and a witness who appears in court against a trades-union, 'must be helped to emigrate.' "

This is, indeed, an extreme view. But it is the view of thousands. The workman is quite as selfish a being as his employer; we cannot credit him with having better motives.

What can the capitalist say for himself? Is he less selfish? Does he love his money less than those whom he employs? Let the long record, especially of British industry, answer. The capitalist has had the advantage of his workman, and he has rarely failed to use it. It is a hard truth that the world is forever trying to get advantage of each other. If all laborers were willing to work for a reasonable, or just price, and all capitalists were willing to pay it; if every exchanger were willing to buy and sell according to the same beautiful rule—the world would move on in perfect harmony. Unhappily, this is not the case. Every man seeks to get the most he can for what he sells, and pay as little as possible for what he buys. This is the law of the world. In order to carry out the law, all are forever inventing methods by which they can overreach each other, while the overreached are continually applying counter-protectives.

If a restrictive tariff law is enacted by which a railroad company pays twenty-five per cent. more for its rails, it makes up the advantage thus accruing to the home manufacturer by raising the price of freights.* If a man intends to buy anything, he hides his real intentions from the seller if he can. Why? Because he fears .the seller will take advantage of the buyer's situation to raise the price. So men hide their real purposes, pretending not to want very badly, although their wants may be great; pretending to be not very desirous of selling, although wishing to sell even at a loss; and thus deceptions are employed; each afraid to tell the honest story of his condition, and trust his fellow, because he knows that, generally, men will take advantage of each other if they can. The capitalist is like the rest, and, unfortunately for the laboring class, he has an advantage over them which it is difficult for them to overcome. He can live if all his capital is not employed in reproduction; their labor will not keep, and, if they are not employed, they perish.

For example: A owns a factory run by a hundred.hands. They demand higher wages and refuse to work until they be given. But the owner says: "No, I will stop my mill first." He has property besides, and can live upon that until it is exhausted; perhaps he has enough for his support always. But if the laborer does not work, he will starve. It is clear enough, then, that A holds his help in the hollow of his hand and can squeeze them as hard as he pleases. This is the fact, and every true observer will say so. Admitting the truth of all the beautiful theorizing about the necessary marriage of labor and capital in order to bring forth fruits for both, capital often has a decided advantage.

The laborer sees this. He says: "The capitalist has a great advantage over me, he can compel me to make a contract by

* See Col. GROSVENOR's admirable article on The Railroads and the Farms, as an illustration. *At. Monthly*, vol. 32, page 591.

which I am not fairly paid for my services." It is like telling a man to deliver up his money or forfeit his life. The capitalist says: "Work for me for so much or I will starve you to death."

And because he has this advantage over the laborer, most capitalists are not slow to avail themselves of it, and this is the cause of the enmity between the two classes.

The laboring class receive more sympathy because they are placed at the greatest disadvantage; they are not, in truth, a whit better than their employers, because, when they become wealthy, as many of them do, they quickly come to see things as other capitalists, and take up practices which once they condemned.

This is not an encouraging view of human nature, though it must be said, lest some one be deceived. Capitalist and laborer, each seeks to do the best he can for himself, each regards his interests as antagonistic to those of the other, each seeks to get every advantage over his opponent, but the capitalist is most favorably situated, he has more advantages, and can generally get the better half of the bargain with the laborer. This is the real situation of both classes.

In making the contract for labor, we maintain that the laborer ought to be willing to work for a reasonable price, and the employer ought to be willing to pay it; and each ought not to take advantage of the situation of the other. If labor be plenty, the employer ought to pay as much, other things with him remaining the same; if scarce, the employed ought to ask no advance of wages, provided his condition in other respects remains unchanged. In short, people ought not to take advantage of each other as they do.

This law men are violating continually. The capitalist declares that, as he is not bound to employ laborers at all, he has the right of paying them any price that may be agreed upon. In other words, as he is independent of the workman, he may pay him as little or as much as he pleases. The plea on behalf of the capitalist has been put by Mr. THORNTON,* in the following form: "Capital, being under no previous obligation to enter into arrangement with labor at all, is at liberty to reject any arrangement to which she objects, and is entitled to whatever profit may accrue to her from any arrangement to which labor and herself mutually agree. That the profit which thus accrues to capital may be fairly regarded as the produce of the labor by which the capital was created and which it represents, and would thus, in the absence of any agreement, belong entirely to capital, for the self-same reason for which unassisted labor is entitled to take as its reward the whole of its own produce." Is it true that the capitalist is under no obligation to enter into agreement with the laborer? Let us examine the question.

What are the relative positions of the two? Let the capitalist cease to employ the laborer, and how much capital has he left? Absolutely nothing. The laborer keeps him from sinking. Dispense with his services, and capital vanishes into thin air. Dispense with labor, and every vessel will rot at the wharves, every farm will run to weeds, the spindle will not give out its music. No man will have anything except what he can get by direct exertion. As for selling his property and living upon the income, who will buy if no labor can be employed? A great factory would not sell for a dollar, because it would be of no more use to the purchaser than the moon. That all desire to preserve their property and enhance its value, is a general truth which no one will deny. Of course, there are spendthrifts who have no ability or

* *On Labor*, page 138.

desire to acquire property, or to keep what they may have inherited. But this is not true of mankind in general. Their desire is
for more wealth, to save what they have and add to its value.
These two facts then being true,—that all are intent upon saving
their property, and that labor is absolutely necessary for this pur-
pose,—the property-owner ought to be willing to pay a fair compensation for the labor whereby his riches are saved and increased.

Now, the usual way of looking at this question is this—no man
is obliged to build a ship, or a factory, in order to employ labor,
because he can loan his money to others. Very true, yet what do
they want of it if they do not employ labor with it? If the manufacturer gets tired of his business and resolves to quit upon the
ground that he is under no obligation to employ any one, he
sells his establishment, and what then? Why, he invests his property in other concerns which employ labor. He employs and pays
for labor less directly; that is the only difference. His money is
put to the same use as before. He buys railroad stocks, but the
railroad employs labor in great quantities. He puts it in a bank,
but the bank employs labor, and loans its capital to others who
use it for the employment of labor. Everywhere capital and labor
touch, and if they do not, one is as worthless as the other.
Whether employed directly, or loaned to others for them to use,
capital must be employed in union with labor, else it is absolutely valueless. The man who is worth a million is as poor as
the man not having a dollar, and both must get a living by
simple and similar tasks. As men will not do that—as they will
use their capital themselves, or loan it to others to be used by
them—they are bound to pay a reasonable reward to the laborer
for his services. The workman is just as necessary a factor in reproduction as capital, and rightfully stands upon an equal plane.

Again, the capitalist asks: "Have I not a right to do what I will with mine own? If I throw my capital away, surely I am under no obligation to employ workmen, for if I am, then all are bound to employ labor, whether having capital or not." If a man has nothing, he cannot be required to employ labor; if he has property, he is bound to use it, either directly or indirectly, for his own support and for the support of others. Can a portion of such property be used as capital in reproducing wealth, then it is a duty he owes to society to employ it so, or spend it in other ways. Government, in protecting property, thus enabling its owner to accumulate more, puts him under obligation to employ a portion of it in reproduction, as well as to spend another portion in the maintenance of himself. He has no right to throw it away. He must use it himself, or loan it to others to be used by them. For, if he will not use it himself or let others use it, his property becomes worthless, and the State is obliged to support him. The State has the right to see that no man wastes his property so as to become a burden to the public.

It is not necessary to go to this extreme length to defend our proposition. The truth is simply this—capital is utterly worthless unless joined with labor. Men are in fact bound to employ labor or else their possessions, whether great or small, are of no value to them or to any one else. Labor is just as necessary a factor in the saving and reproduction of capital, as in producing capital in the first place. Let it not be forgotten that in this whole discussion we are not talking of anything but labor, present and accumulated. Accumulated labor, to be worth anything, must be united with present labor; the two operate together. Consequently, the assertion is without foundation that the capitalist is under no obligation to employ labor. Such an obligation does exist. He has no right to throw his property away. We assume that every man is desirous of saving his property; if so, he must employ labor, else his property becomes valueless. And if he must employ labor to save it, he ought to pay a fair compensation therefor. Suppose a man's house was in danger of being carried away by a flood, and some men coming along were asked to help in saving it. They have no time to make a definite bargain as to the remuneration, but engage with a hearty will, and by their efforts save the house. Would not every one say that the owner of that house was mean if he were not willing to pay those men a reasonable compensation for their services? The position of the capitalist is the same in respect to his property. His capital will vanish like a stroke of lightning unless united with labor. Analyze the uses made of capital, and all cannot help admitting the fact. Labor is necessary to save property and enhance its value; if the owners of lands, factories, etc., are desirous of securing these ends, they must employ labor. Therefore they ought to pay a reasonable price for it.

As between workmen, there is a natural difference; one man is worth more than another, because he has greater strength or skill. It is right that the strongest and most skillful should receive higher wages. Concerning these natural advantages, there is nothing to be said. What we object to is the use of artificial and wrongful advantage. If the corn crop is less this year, the price should not be increased, except to require people to practice economy, or for some other good reason. If laborers are plentiful, let them be paid as much; if they are scarce, let them work for the old prices. Let no advantage be taken of unnatural, artificial, or forced conditions, and all will be well.

It will be said that this mode of reasoning is contrary to the operation of supply and demand. Shall that law cease to be applied? No, not in the true sense. All that we have written about asking and expecting reasonable prices, does not conflict with the working of this law. There is, however, a wide difference between the natural and unnatural operation of supply and demand. Rightly interpreted, the law is this—demand is what people really need and would purchase if they could buy at a reasonable price; and supply is the quantity that can be had at such a price. But the world is forever interfering with this law, by creating artificial scarcity on the one hand, and, on the other, by trying to make the demand less than it really is, so as to beat down the price. The law, to a great extent, does not express the truth about exchanges. The real demand is often much greater than purchases indicate, and the supply also. But people deceive each other; they exercise force, they refuse to sell when they really want to, hoping for an advance of prices. The buyer refuses to buy, although he really wants the thing, hoping to get a reduction of price. So numerous are the deceptions practiced, the real state of things is covered up so deeply, that the natural law of demand and supply has, in fact, only a limited operation.

What is a reasonable price depends upon many things. Obviously, it is impossible to draw any hard and fast line defining it. The most we can do is to find out what principle should govern in making contracts between capitalist and workman. This is a reasonable price without regard to any advantage which either capitalist or laborer might take of the condition of the other.

There are some considerations, however, that may be mentioned in making contracts for labor. First, the laborer should receive more where the work is hazardous to life and health, than in those occupations which are healthy and free from accident. An operative in a powder mill, or who makes certain parts of a brimstone match, ought to receive higher wages than a person working in a woolen factory, which is comparatively healthy and safe. Secondly, a person ought not to expect so much who receives regular employment as a person who cannot get work regularly. The ordinary hackman is justified in charging more for conveying passengers, if he can get them only now and then, than if he were employed all the time. The same person will charge less by the hour if he is to be employed for several hours, than if employed to go a short distance, in proportion to the time required. This is just. With a great many who work in factories, especially in New England, they ought not to expect so much, because their employers, in most instances, feel bound to give them constant employment if possible. Ofttimes they run, and at a loss, when they would not run, except to keep their help employed. Other considerations of less importance probably enter into the contract fixing the price of wages.

There are some subsidiary questions surrounding the main one which require notice. It is said, that labor is paid enough generally, whatever the price may be, because, as a class, workmen do not make a wise use of their wages.

That workmen are often prodigal in the use of their wages will not be denied. Since the war, the wages of factory operatives have remained nearly the same as before, the prices of living have been reduced, consequently operatives have reaped a fine harvest. Some of them have saved their money, though the larger number have spent it all. The goods in the factory stores and villages have changed in many respects, which is the best proof of the extravagance of this class. The amount of jewelry they wear is very large and expensive to what it was a few years ago. Their clothing, also, is costlier, and their living as well.

Now, it is said, why pay them so much? they do not make an economic use of their money; teach them to use it properly before giving it to them. This, by way of advice, is good. Operatives spend a great deal of money foolishly, and they should be taught to save it against a day of want, and for nobler uses. Yet is this a good defence to paying them higher wages?

The same mode of arguing will cut the manufacturer off from making money, for does he put it to any better use than his operatives? Is he not as extravagant, does he not spend as much money foolishly? He cannot, in truth, say anything on that score.

Thus we have gone over the ground between the capitalist and laborer, and sought to find out what is the true rule in the payment of labor. We do not say that the fixing of any price is always best; a division of the profits upon some agreed plan is preferable, whenever a division is practicable. It is not practicable in every case, and when it is not, this rule has a decided preference over every other. How various plans for rewarding labor have succeeded, and what efforts workmen have made to increase the price of wages, will be considered in the next chapter.

This concludes Chapters I and II. The remaining books can be ordered from Amazon.com by searching on any of the following titles.

www.ingramcontent.com/pod-product-compliance
Lightning Source LLC
Chambersburg PA
CBHW060707280326
41933CB00012B/2333